Sisters

A Record Book About Us

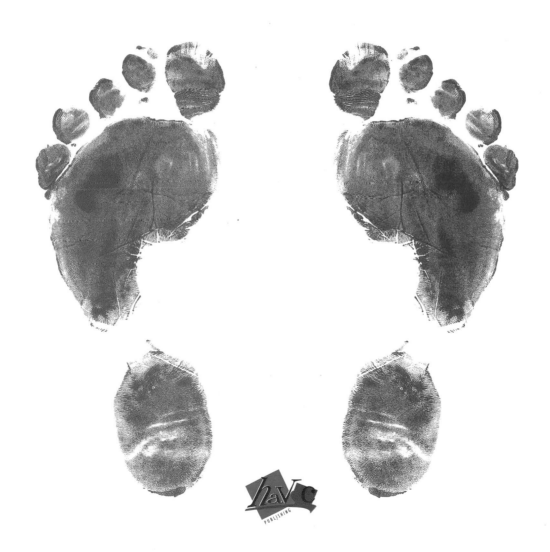

havoc
PUBLISHING

© 1997 Havoc Publishing

ISBN 1-57977-100-9

Published and created by Havoc Publishing

San Diego, California

First Printing, May 1997

Designed by Juddesign

Some images © 1997 PhotoDisc, Inc.

Printed in China

Please write to us for more information on our
Havoc Publishing Record Books and Products.

HAVOC PUBLISHING

7868 Silverton Avenue, Suite A

San Diego, California 92126

Sisters

A Record Book About Us

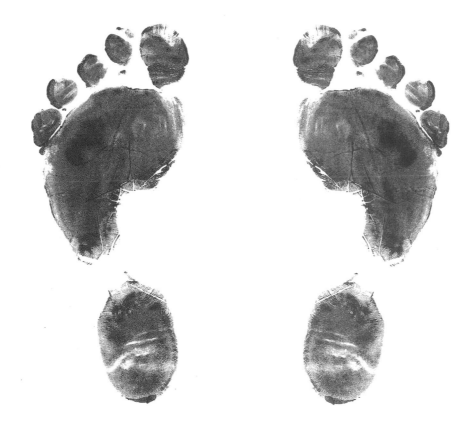

This book is dedicated to the friendship of sisters

_____ _____

Contents

Contents

It's All in the Jeans

Features we share _____

Our unique features _____

_____

_____

What feature I would gladly trade with you _____

What feature you would gladly trade with me _____

My picture

Your picture

Earliest memories of you

_____

_____

_____

_____

Family memories

_____

_____

_____

_____

Where we grew up

_____

_____

_____

_____

Birthdays . . .

You were born on

I was born on

and this is what you looked like:

and this is what I looked like:

Paste baby pic here

Paste baby pic here

Big Sister, Little Sister

Favorite parties, when & where

_____

_____

_____

_____

Friends who attended

_____

_____

_____

_____

Other memorable celebrations

_____

_____

_____

_____

SCHOOL DAYS

Schools we attended

School friends

Our favorite teachers

Not-so favorite teachers

School pic here

School pic here

Most embarrassing school
experience

All about school dances (sigh!)

Most hilarious school
experience

Official (and unofficial) ditch
days

Baggin' It

Cafeteria horror stories

What Mom always packed us

Different Tastes

My favorite foods
_____

_____

_____

_____

Your favorite foods
_____

_____

_____

Our favorite restaurants
_____

_____

_____

Our favorite restaurant story
_____

_____

_____

_____

_____

_____

Our favorite take-out
_____

_____

_____

_____

"Drink Your Milk"
& Other Mom-isms

Mom's pic

What we absolutely hated that
Mom made us do

What we absolutely loved
to do that Mom hated

Clean up your room • Stand up straight • Don't do that to your sister • Time to go to bed • Eat your vegetables • Stop fighting • You could poke an eye out with that • Share • Listen to your father • Did you do your homework • Quit playing with your food • Brush your teeth • Go play

Lowfat Milk
2% Milkfat Vitamins A&D
...ized

right up
here

Photograph

And in This Corner...

Busted!

Who won the fights

_____

_____

_____

_____

Most memorable fight

_____

_____

_____

_____

_____

I told on you for . . .

_____

_____

_____

Most ridiculous fight

_____

_____

_____

_____

Emotional Water Works

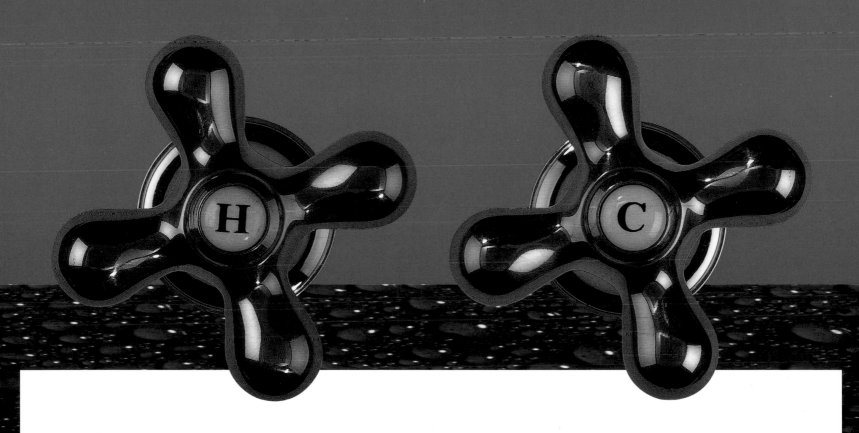

What makes you laugh

What makes you cry

What I had to do
_____
_____
_____
_____
_____
_____

The worst chores
_____
_____
_____
_____

The best chores
_____
_____
_____

What you had to do
_____
_____
_____
_____
_____
_____

Best way to get out of chores
_____
_____
_____
_____
_____

The Chores

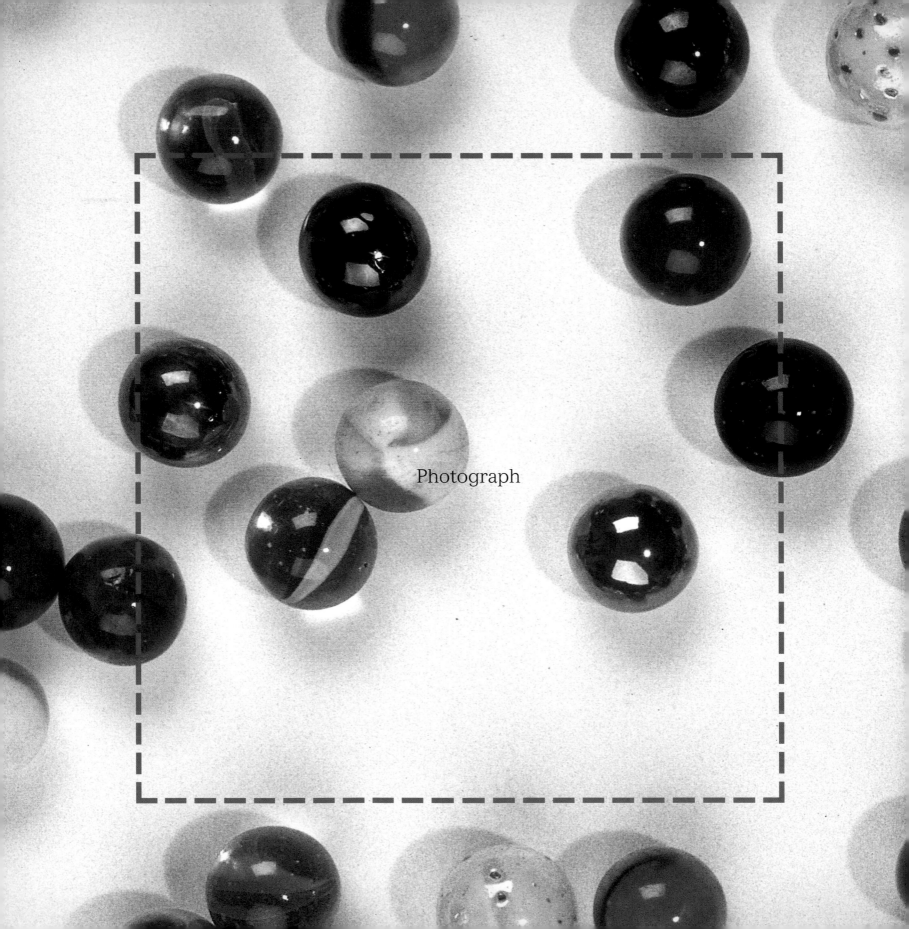
Photograph

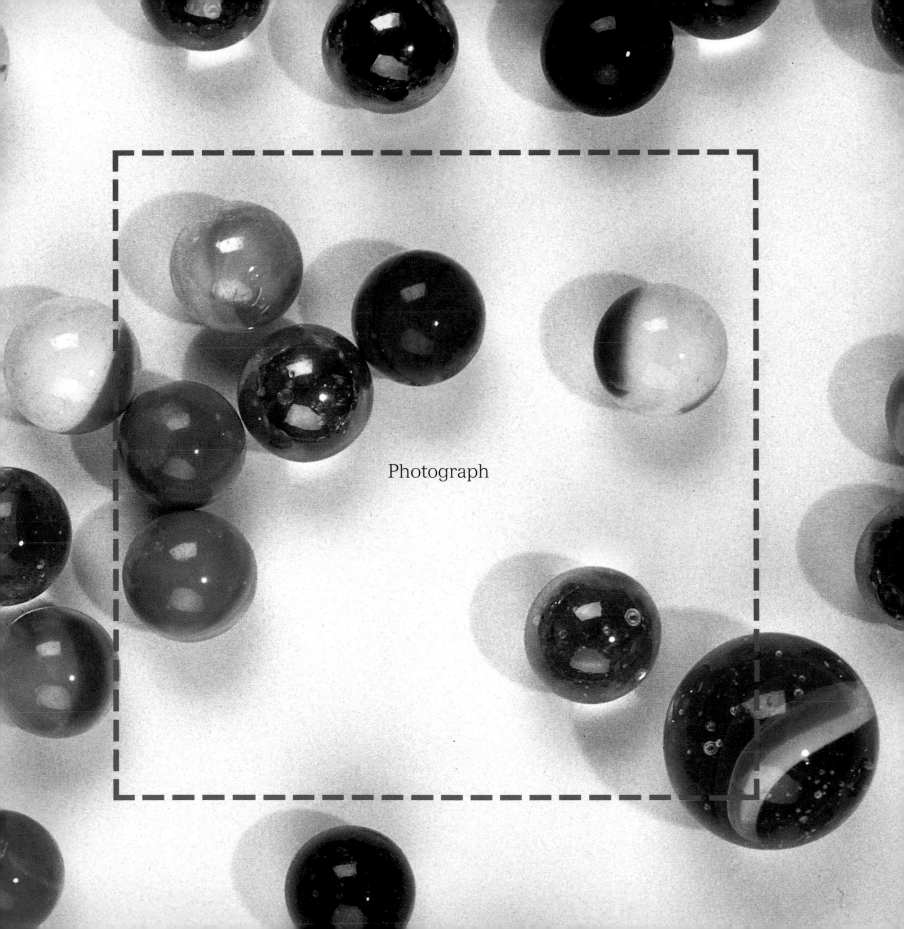

Photograph

Holidays & Festivities

Funniest Family Story

Pet Peeves

Our family pets

_____

_____

_____

_____

Our most unusual pets

_____

_____

_____

_____

About our pets

_____

_____

_____

The most memorable pet stories

_____

_____

_____

The most pets we ever had at one time

_____

_____

_____

Go ♥ mes

Stories about my sister _____   Things we grew to like about each other _____

_____   _____

_____   _____

_____   _____

_____   _____

_____   _____

_____   _____

_____   _____

_____   _____

_____   _____

_____   _____

_____   _____

_____   _____

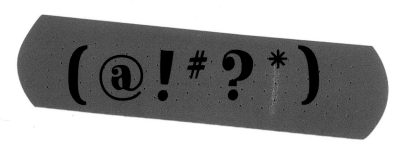

Favorite play-time activities

_____

_____

_____

Favorite playmates

_____

_____

_____

Favorite parks and places we liked to go

_____

_____

_____

Memorable bumps and bruises

_____

_____

_____

Photograph

Things only you understood

The strangest thing that ever happened to us

sooooooooo bizarre!

Sisterly Quirks

We always laugh when we think about

_____

_____

_____

_____

_____

_____

_____

Secrets

Best kept secrets

Secrets that accidentally became public (oops!)

Your reactions

My reactions

In Your Face

Issues you feel strongly about

Issues we agree about

Issues I feel strongly about

Issues we disagree about

Seeing   to

E
C B
D L F
P T E O
F Z B D E
O F L C T B
T P E O L F D Z

The best advice you ever gave me
_____

_____

_____

_____

The worst advice you ever gave me
_____

_____

_____

_____

Why I still listen to you
_____

_____

_____

_____

_____

A sister is both your mirror - and
your opposite.   *Elizabeth Fishel*

Mirror Mirror . . .

Beautiful things about my sister

_____
_____
_____
_____
_____
_____
_____
_____
_____
_____
_____

Funniest story

_____
_____
_____
_____
_____

Who spent the most time primping

_____
_____
_____
_____

Discovering Make-Up

Make-up fiascos

Dress up nightmares

Rites of Passage

All About Men

YEAH! The person I most approved of in
your romantic life and why

_____

_____

_____

_____

_____

YUCK! The person I least liked that you
were involved with and why

_____

_____

_____

_____

_____

The best

photo

K ♥ / K ♥

The worst

JOKER / JOKER

photo

He Loves Me, He Loves Me Not . . .

He loves me

He loves me not

He loves me

He loves me not

He loves me

He loves me

He loves me not

Loves and crushes

He loves me not

He loves me

He loves me not

The Phone Fiascos

Fights over the phone

Will You Get Off the Phone!?!

The longest phone calls

The Clothing Issue

Who got the ol' hand-me-downs

Our different styles

Photograph

Photograph

I Was So Proud of You When . . .

_____

_____

_____

_____

_____

_____

_____

_____

_____

_____

_____

_____

_____

I Have an Announcement to Make

I missed you most
_____
_____
_____
_____
_____

You were there for me
_____
_____
_____
_____

You pushed me in the right direction
_____
_____
_____
_____

hot summers

things in spring

chilly

w i n t e r s

f a l l
shopping

Yours

Types of music _____

_____

Singers _____

Groups _____

Mine

Types of music _____

_____

Singers _____

Groups _____

Favorite Tunes

Your favorite TV shows

_____

_____

_____

_____

My favorite TV shows

_____

_____

_____

_____

Tales of the well-Traveled

Family trips
_____
_____
_____
_____
_____
_____

Places we traveled as children
_____
_____
_____

Places we traveled as adults
_____
_____
_____

Adventures Just Between Us

_____

_____

_____

_____

_____

_____

_____

_____

_____

_____

_____

_____

_____

_____

They could see she was a real princess and no question about

it, now that she had felt **one pea all** the way through twenty

mattresses and **twenty more** feather beds. Nobody but a

princess could be **so delicate**. – Hans Christian Andersen

(The Princess and the Pea)

Like Two Peas in a Pod

How we are alike

_____

_____

_____

How we are different

_____

_____

_____

Stuff we like to do just the two of us

_____

_____

_____

What I wish for you

_____

_____

_____

Your Goals

_____

_____

_____

_____

My Goals

_____

_____

_____

_____

_____

_____

ere We   selves Later

_____

_____

_____

_____

_____

_____

_____

_____

_____

_____

_____

_____

Available Record Books
from Havoc

Animal Antics - Cats

Animal Antics - Dogs

Couples

Girlfriends

Golf

Grandmother

Our Honeymoon

Mom

Sisters

Tying the Knot

Traveling Adventures

Please write to us with your ideas for additional
Havoc Publishing Record Books and Products

HAVOC PUBLISHING
7868 Silverton Avenue, Suite A
San Diego, California 92126